UKULELE

NEIL YOUNG GREATEST HITS

INCLUDING:

DOWN BY THE RIVER...PAGE 3

COWGIRL IN THE SAND...PAGE 7

CINNAMON GIRL...PAGE 11

HELPLESS...PAGE 17

AFTER THE GOLD RUSH...PAGE 21

ONLY LOVE CAN BREAK YOUR HEART...PAGE 24

SOUTHERN MAN...PAGE 28

OHIO...PAGE 33

THE NEEDLE & THE DAMAGE DONE...PAGE 37

OLD MAN...PAGE 41

HEART OF GOLD...PAGE 46

LIKE A HURRICANE...PAGE 51

COMES A TIME...PAGE 55

HEY HEY MY MY (INTO THE BLACK)...PAGE 58

ROCKIN' IN THE FREE WORLD...PAGE 63

HARVEST MOON...PAGE 68

ISBN: 978-1-4584-9119-0

HAL•LEONARD®
CORPORATION

7777 W. BLUEMOUND RD. P.O. BOX 13819 MILWAUKEE, WI 53213

In Australia Contact: **Hal Leonard Australia Pty. Ltd.** 4 Lentara Court, Cheltenham, Victoria, 3192 Australia Email: ausadmin@halleonard.com.au
Visit Hal Leonard Online at **www.halleonard.com**

DOWN BY THE RIVER

BE ON MY SIDE, I'LL BE ON YOUR SIDE
THERE IS NO REASON FOR YOU TO HIDE
IT'S SO HARD FOR ME STAYING HERE ALL ALONE
WHEN YOU COULD BE TAKING ME FOR A RIDE
SHE COULD DRAG ME OVER THE RAINBOW
AND SEND ME AWAY

DOWN BY THE RIVER
I SHOT MY BABY
DOWN BY THE RIVER
DEAD
(OOH, SHOT HER DEAD)

YOU TAKE MY HAND, I'LL TAKE YOUR HAND
TOGETHER WE MAY GET AWAY
THIS MUCH MADNESS IS TOO MUCH SORROW
IT'S IMPOSSIBLE TO MAKE IT TODAY

SHE COULD DRAG ME OVER THE RAINBOW
AND SEND ME AWAY
DOWN BY THE RIVER
I SHOT MY BABY
DOWN BY THE RIVER
DEAD,
(DEAD, OOOH, OOOH
SHOT HER DEAD...SHOT HER DEAD)

BE ON MY SIDE, I'LL BE ON YOUR SIDE
THERE IS NO REASON FOR YOU TO HIDE
IT'S SO HARD FOR ME STAYING HERE ALL ALONE
WHEN YOU COULD BE TAKING ME FOR A RIDE

SHE COULD DRAG ME OVER THE RAINBOW
AND SEND ME AWAY
DOWN BY THE RIVER...I SHOT MY BABY
DOWN BY THE RIVER

(REPEAT)

Down by the River

Words and Music by Neil Young

Additional Lyrics

2. You take my hand, I'll take your hand,
Together we may get away.
This much madness is too much sorrow,
It's impossible to make it today,
Yeah, ooh, ooh, yeah.
She could drag me over the rainbow
And send me away.

EVERYBODY KNOWS THIS IS NOWHERE

NEIL YOUNG

COWGIRL IN THE SAND

HELLO, COWGIRL IN THE SAND
IS THIS PLACE AT YOUR COMMAND?
CAN I STAY HERE FOR A WHILE?
CAN I SEE YOUR SWEET, SWEET SMILE?

OLD ENOUGH NOW TO CHANGE YOUR NAME
WHEN SO MANY LOVE YOU, IS IT THE SAME?
IT'S THE WOMAN IN YOU THAT MAKES YOU WANT TO PLAY THIS GAME

HELLO, RUBY IN THE DUST
HAS YOUR BAND BEGUN TO RUST?
AFTER ALL THE SIN WE'VE HAD
I WAS HOPING THAT WE'D TURN BAD

OLD ENOUGH TO CHANGE YOUR NAME
WHEN SO MANY LOVE YOU, IS IT THE SAME?
IT'S THE WOMAN IN YOU THAT MAKES YOU WANT TO PLAY THIS GAME

HELLO, WOMAN OF MY DREAMS
IS THIS NOT THE WAY IT SEEMS?
PURPLE WORDS ON A GRAY BACKGROUND
TO BE A WOMAN AND TO BE TURNED DOWN

OLD ENOUGH NOW TO CHANGE YOUR NAME
WHEN SO MANY LOVE YOU, IS IT THE SAME?
IT'S THE WOMAN IN YOU THAT MAKES YOU WANT TO PLAY THIS GAME

COWGIRL IN THE SAND

HELLO, COWGIRL IN THE SAND
IS THIS PLACE AT YOUR COMMAND?
CAN I STAY HERE FOR A WHILE?
CAN I SEE YOUR SWEET, SWEET SMILE?

OLD ENOUGH NOW TO CHANGE YOUR NAME
WHEN SO MANY LOVE YOU, IS IT THE SAME?
IT'S THE WOMAN IN YOU THAT MAKES YOU WANT TO PLAY THIS GAME

HELLO, RUBY IN THE DUST
HAS YOUR BAND BEGUN TO RUST?
AFTER ALL THE SIN WE'VE HAD
I WAS HOPING THAT WE'D TURN BAD

OLD ENOUGH TO CHANGE YOUR NAME
WHEN SO MANY LOVE YOU, IS IT THE SAME?
IT'S THE WOMAN IN YOU THAT MAKES YOU WANT TO PLAY THIS GAME

HELLO, WOMAN OF MY DREAMS
IS THIS NOT THE WAY IT SEEMS?
PURPLE WORDS ON A GRAY BACKGROUND
TO BE A WOMAN AND TO BE TURNED DOWN

OLD ENOUGH NOW TO CHANGE YOUR NAME
WHEN SO MANY LOVE YOU, IS IT THE SAME?
IT'S THE WOMAN IN YOU THAT MAKES YOU WANT TO PLAY THIS GAME

Cowgirl in the Sand

Words and Music by Neil Young

First note

Verse
Moderately slow

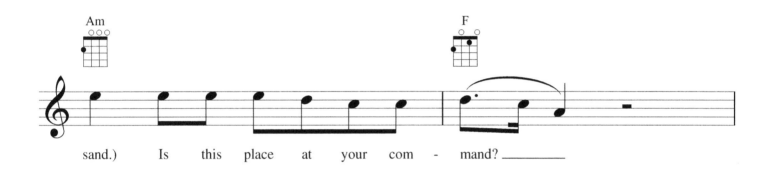

1. Hel - lo, cow - girl in the sand. (Hel - lo, cow - girl in the
2., 3. *See additional lyrics*

sand.) Is this place at your com - mand? _____

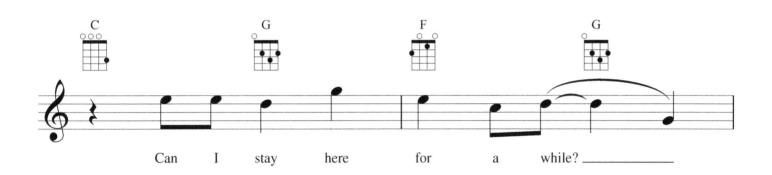

Can I stay here for a while? _____

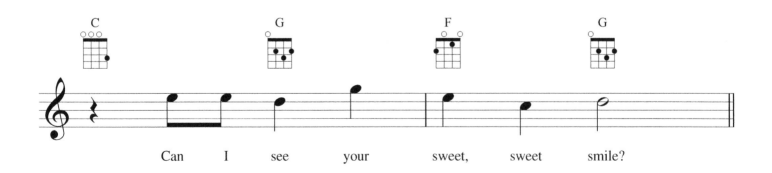

Can I see your sweet, sweet smile?

Chorus

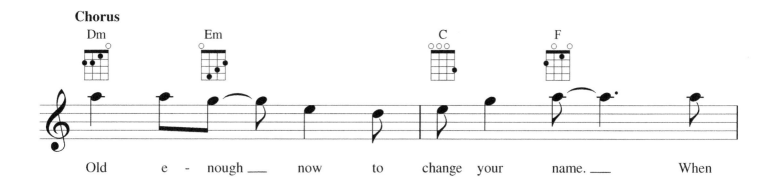

Old   e - nough ___   now   to   change   your   name. ___   When

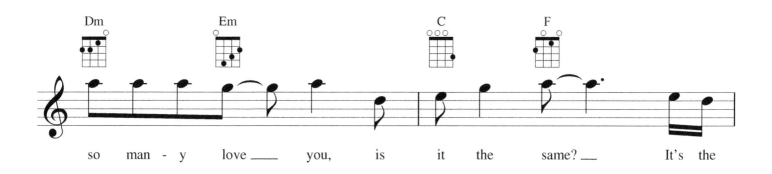

so   man - y   love ___   you,   is   it   the   same? ___   It's   the

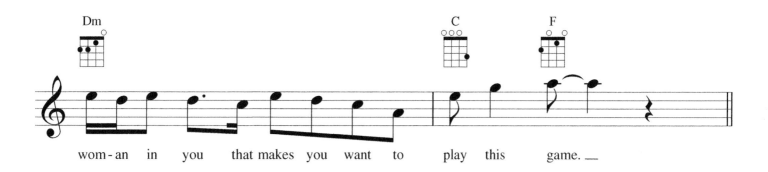

wom - an   in   you   that makes   you   want   to   play   this   game. ___

Interlude

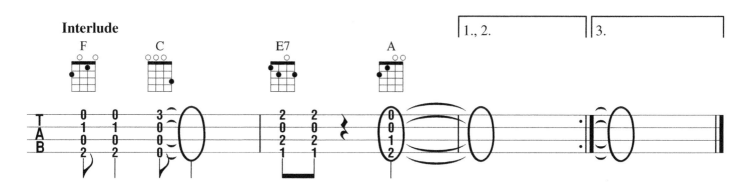

Additional Lyrics

2. Hello, ruby in the dust. (Hello, ruby in the dust.)
   Has your band begun to rust?
   After all the sin we've had,
   I was hoping that we'd turn bad.

3. Hello, woman of my dreams. (Hello, woman of my dreams.)
   Is this not the way it seems?
   Purple words on a gray background,
   To be a woman and to be turned down.

CINNAMON GIRL

I WANT TO LIVE WITH A CINNAMON GIRL
I COULD BE HAPPY THE REST OF MY LIFE
WITH A CINNAMON GIRL

A DREAMER OF PICTURES
I RUN IN THE NIGHT
YOU SEE US TOGETHER
CHASING THE MOONLIGHT
MY CINNAMON GIRL

TEN SILVER SAXES
A BASS WITH A BOW
THE DRUMMER RELAXES
AND WAITS BETWEEN SHOWS
FOR HIS CINNAMON GIRL

A DREAMER OF PICTURES
I RUN IN THE NIGHT
YOU SEE US TOGETHER
CHASING THE MOONLIGHT
MY CINNAMON GIRL

MA SEND ME MONEY NOW
I'M GONNA MAKE IT SOMEHOW
I NEED ANOTHER CHANCE
YOU SEE YOUR BABY LOVES TO DANCE
YEAH
YEAH
YEAH

Cinnamon Girl

Words and Music by Neil Young

First note

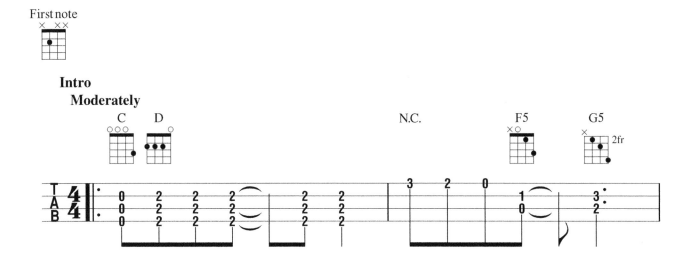

Intro
Moderately

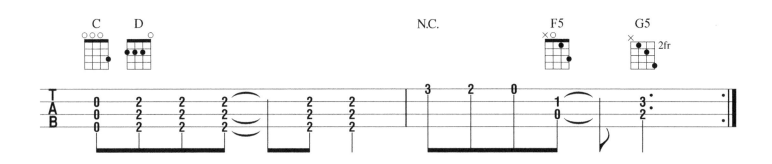

Verse

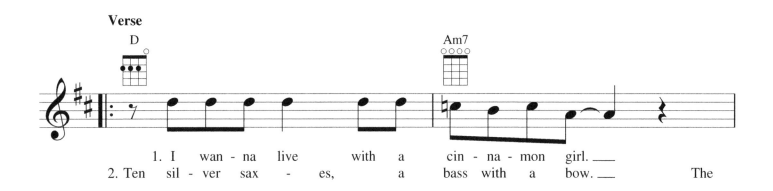

1. I wan-na live with a cin-na-mon girl. ___
2. Ten sil-ver sax - es, a bass with a bow. ___ The

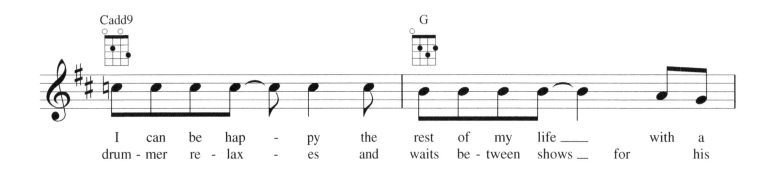

I can be hap-py the rest of my life ____ with a
drum-mer re-lax - es and waits be-tween shows ___ for his

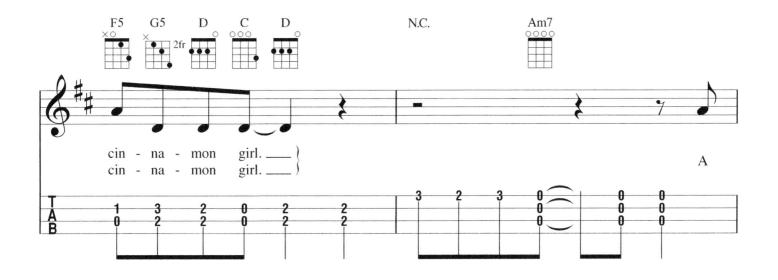

cin - na - mon girl. ____

cin - na - mon girl. ____

A

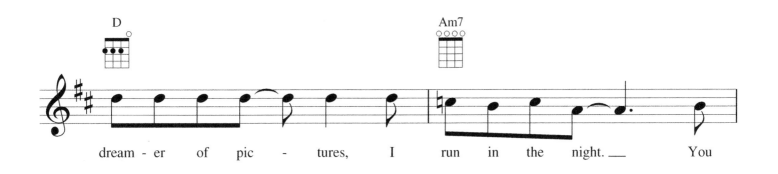

dream - er of pic - tures, I run in the night. ____ You

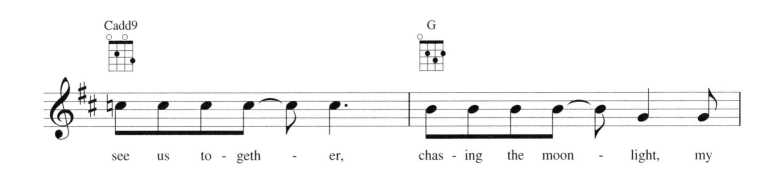

see us to - geth - er, chas - ing the moon - light, my

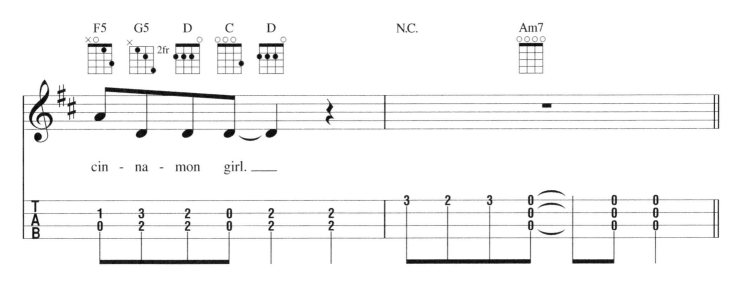

cin - na - mon girl. ____

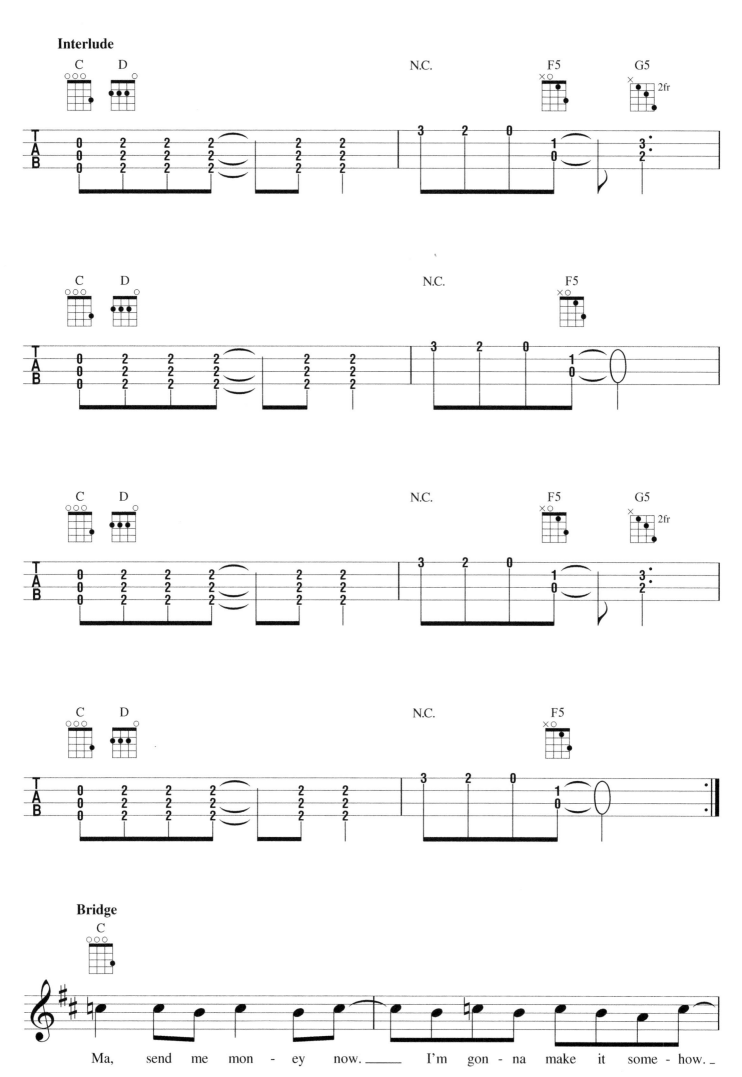

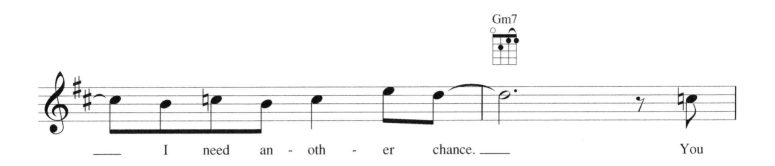

_____ I need an - oth - er chance. _____ You

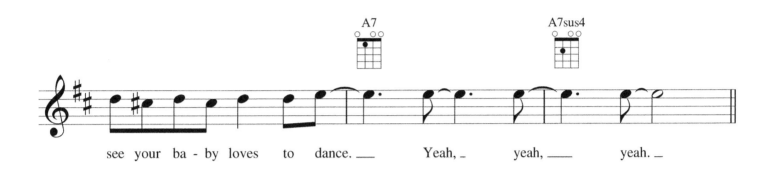

see your ba - by loves to dance. ___ Yeah, _ yeah, ___ yeah. _

Outro

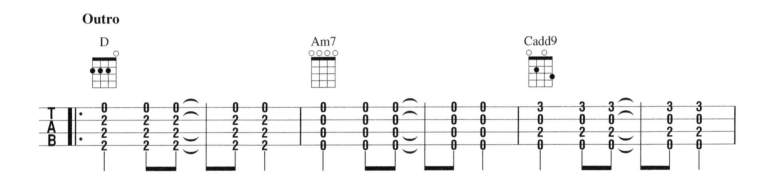

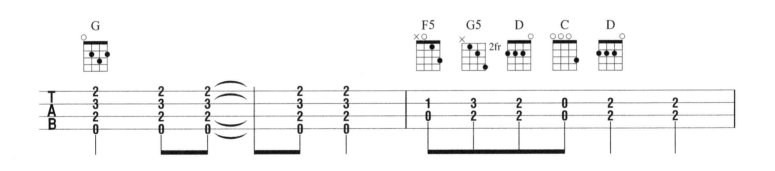

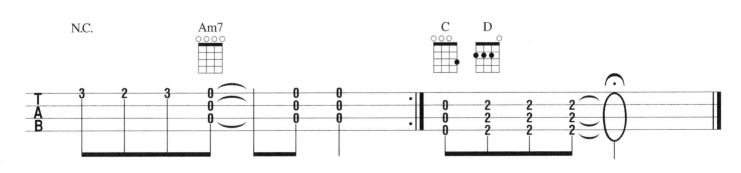

HELPLESS

THERE IS A TOWN IN NORTH ONTARIO
WITH DREAM COMFORT MEMORY TO SPARE
AND IN MY MIND I STILL NEED A PLACE TO GO
ALL MY CHANGES WERE THERE

BLUE BLUE WINDOWS BEHIND THE STARS
YELLOW MOON ON THE RISE
BIG BIRDS FLYING ACROSS THE SKY
THROWING SHADOWS ON OUR EYES
LEAVE US

HELPLESS
BABE CAN YOU HEAR ME NOW
THE CHAINS ARE LOCKED AND TIED ACROSS THE DOOR
BABE SING WITH ME SOMEHOW

BLUE BLUE WINDOWS BEHIND THE STARS
YELLOW MOON ON THE RISE
BIG BIRDS FLYING ACROSS THE SKY
THROWING SHADOWS ON OUR EYES

Helpless

Words and Music by Neil Young

Ba - by, can you hear me now?

The chains _____ are locked and tied a - cross the door.

D.C. al Coda
(take 2nd ending)

Ba - by, sing _____ with me some - how. _____

Coda
Outro

help - less, help - less, help - less.

Repeat and fade

Help - less, help - less, help - less.

Additional Lyrics

2., 3. Blue, blue windows behind the stars,
Yellow moon on the rise,
Big birds flying across the sky,
Throwing shadows on our eyes leave us...

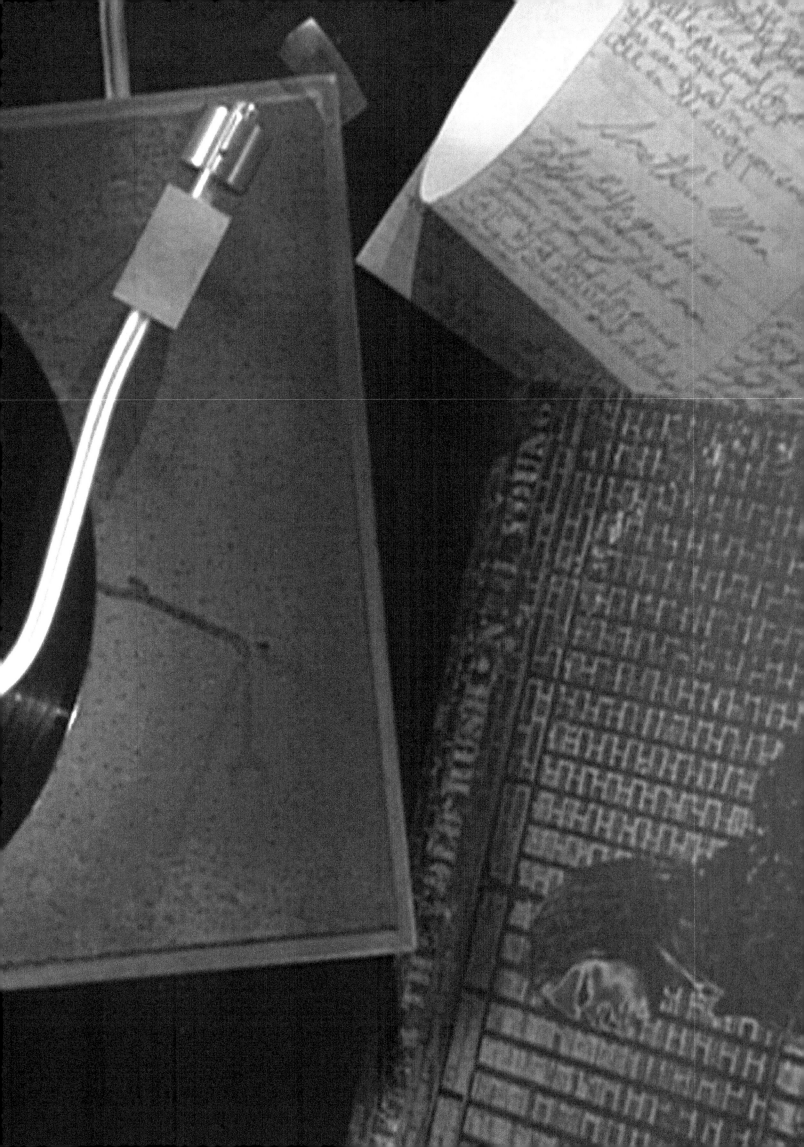

AFTER THE GOLD RUSH

WELL I DREAMED I SAW THE KNIGHTS IN ARMOR COMING
SAYING SOMETHING ABOUT A QUEEN
THERE WERE PEASANTS SINGING AND DRUMMERS DRUMMING
AND THE ARCHER SPLIT THE TREE
THERE WAS A FANFARE BLOWING TO THE SUN
THAT WAS FLOATING ON THE BREEZE

LOOK AT MOTHER NATURE ON THE RUN IN THE 1970'S
LOOK AT MOTHER NATURE ON THE RUN IN THE 1970'S

I WAS LYING IN A BURNED-OUT BASEMENT
WITH THE FULL MOON IN MY EYE
I WAS HOPING FOR REPLACEMENT
WHEN THE SUN BURST THROUGH THE SKY
THERE WAS A BAND PLAYING IN MY HEAD
AND I FELT LIKE GETTING HIGH

I WAS THINKING ABOUT WHAT A FRIEND HAD SAID
I WAS HOPING IT WAS A LIE
THINKING ABOUT WHAT A FRIEND HAD SAID
I WAS HOPING IT WAS A LIE

WELL I DREAMED I SAW THE SILVER SPACESHIPS FLYING
IN THE YELLOW HAZE OF THE SUN
THERE WERE CHILDREN CRYING AND COLORS FLYING
ALL AROUND THE CHOSEN ONES
ALL IN A DREAM, ALL IN A DREAM THE LOADING HAD BEGUN

FLYING MOTHER NATURE'S SILVER SEED TO A NEW HOME IN THE SUN
FLYING MOTHER NATURE'S SILVER SEED TO A NEW HOME

After the Gold Rush

Words and Music by Neil Young

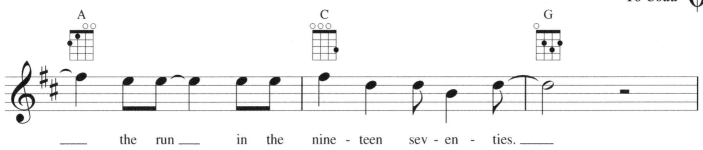

_____ the run _____ in the nine - teen sev - en - ties. _____

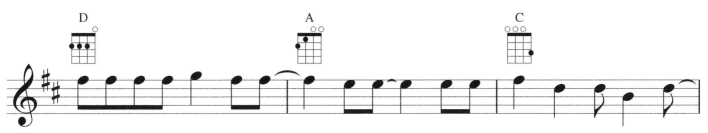

Look at Moth-er Na - ture on _____ the run _____ in the nine - teen sev - en - ties. _

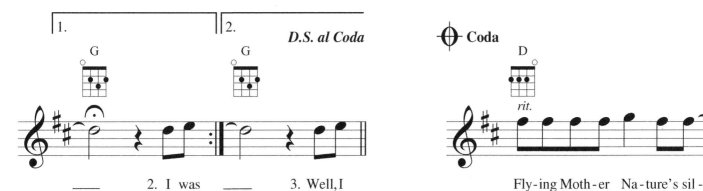

1. **2.**

D.S. al Coda   ⊕ **Coda**

_____ 2. I was _____ 3. Well, I   Fly-ing Moth-er Na-ture's sil -

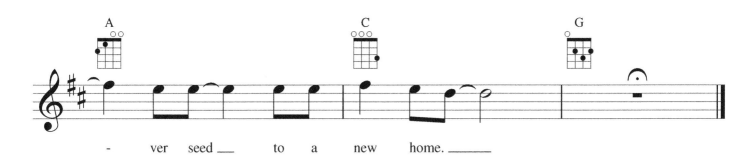

- ver seed _____ to a new home. _____

Additional Lyrics

2. I was lying in a burned-out basement
   With the full moon in my eye.
   I was hopin' for replacement when the sun burst through the sky.
   There was a band playin' in my head,
   And I felt like getting high.
   I was thinkin' about what a friend had said, I was hopin' it was a lie.
   Thinkin' about what a friend had said, I was hopin' it was a lie.

3. Well, I dreamed I saw the silver spaceships flyin'
   In the yellow haze of the sun.
   There were children cryin' and colors flyin' all around the chosen ones.
   All in a dream, all in a dream
   The loading had begun.
   Flying Mother Nature's silver seed to a new home in the sun.
   Flying Mother Nature's silver seed to a new home.

ONLY LOVE CAN BREAK YOUR HEART

WHEN YOU WERE YOUNG AND ON YOUR OWN
HOW DID IT FEEL TO BE ALONE
I WAS ALWAYS THINKING OF GAMES THAT I WAS PLAYING
TRYING TO MAKE THE BEST OF MY TIME

BUT ONLY LOVE CAN BREAK YOUR HEART
TRY TO BE SURE RIGHT FROM THE START
YES, ONLY LOVE CAN BREAK YOUR HEART
WHAT IF YOUR WORLD SHOULD FALL APART

I HAVE A FRIEND I'VE NEVER SEEN
HE HIDES HIS HEAD INSIDE A DREAM
SOMEONE SHOULD CALL HIM AND SEE IF HE CAN COME OUT
TRY TO LOSE THE DOWN THAT HE'S FOUND

BUT ONLY LOVE CAN BREAK YOUR HEART
TRY TO BE SURE RIGHT FROM THE START
YES, ONLY LOVE CAN BREAK YOUR HEART
WHAT IF YOUR WORLD SHOULD FALL APART

I HAVE A FRIEND I'VE NEVER SEEN
HE HIDES HIS HEAD INSIDE A DREAM
YES, ONLY LOVE CAN BREAK YOUR HEART
(REPEAT)

Only Love Can Break Your Heart

Words and Music by Neil Young

First note

Verse
Moderately

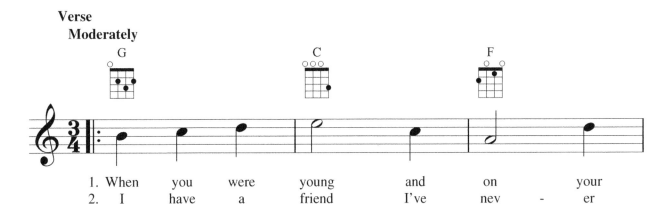

1. When you were young and on your
2. I have a friend and I've nev - er

own, how did it feel to
seen, he did hides his head to in -

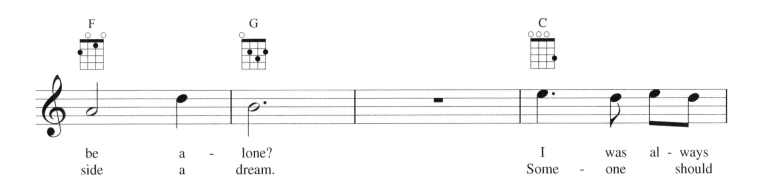

be a - lone? I was al - ways
side a dream. Some - one should

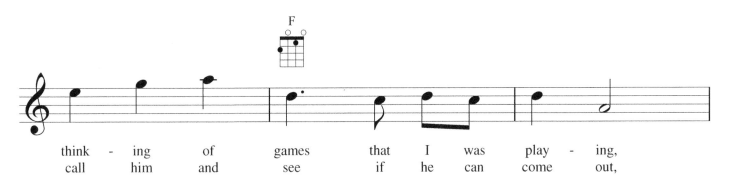

think - ing of games that I was play - ing,
call him and see if he can come out,

try - ing to make the best of my time.
try to lose the down that he's found.

Chorus

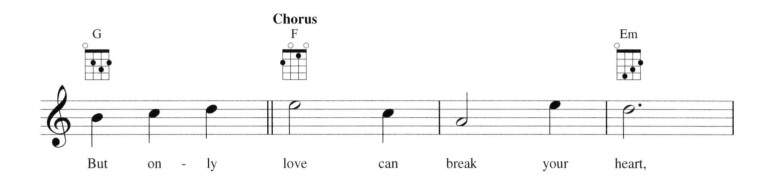

But on - ly love can break your heart,

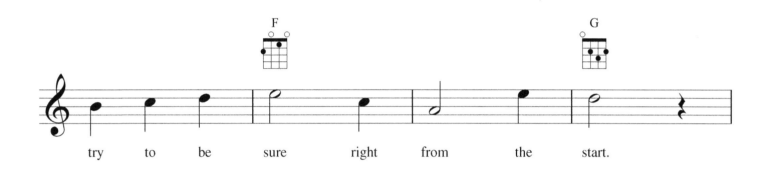

try to be sure right from the start.

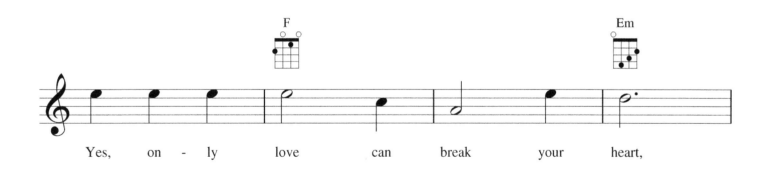

Yes, on - ly love can break your heart,

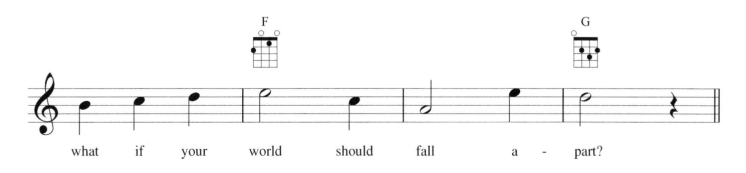

what if your world should fall a - part?

Interlude

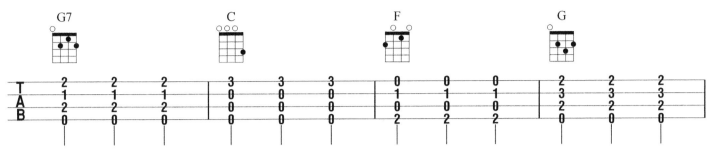

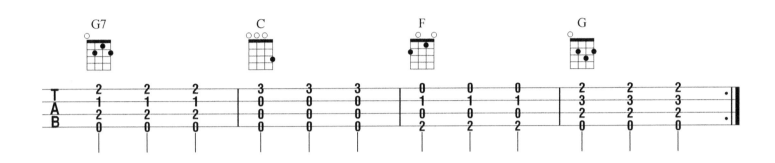

Outro-Verse

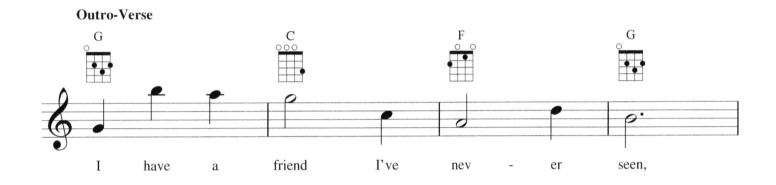

I have a friend I've nev - er seen,

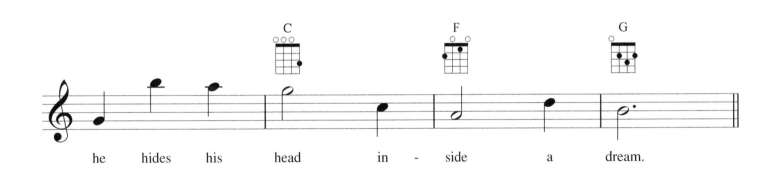

he hides his head in - side a dream.

Repeat and fade

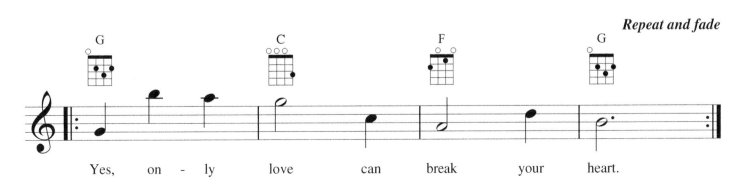

Yes, on - ly love can break your heart.

SOUTHERN MAN

SOUTHERN MAN BETTER KEEP YOUR HEAD
DON'T FORGET WHAT YOUR GOOD BOOK SAID
SOUTHERN CHANGE GONNA COME AT LAST
NOW YOUR CROSSES ARE BURNING FAST
SOUTHERN MAN

I SAW COTTON AND I SAW BLACK
TALL WHITE MANSIONS AND LITTLE SHACKS
SOUTHERN MAN WHEN WILL YOU PAY THEM BACK
I HEARD SCREAMIN' AND BULLWHIPS CRACKIN'
HOW LONG, HOW LONG

SOUTHERN MAN BETTER KEEP YOUR HEAD
DON'T FORGET WHAT YOUR GOOD BOOK SAID
SOUTHERN CHANGE GONNA COME AT LAST
NOW YOUR CROSSES ARE BURNING FAST
SOUTHERN MAN

LILY BELLE, YOUR HAIR IS GOLDEN BROWN
I'VE SEEN YOUR BLACK MAN COMING 'ROUND
SWEAR BY GOD I'M GONNA CUT HIM DOWN
I HEARD SCREAMIN' AND BULLWHIPS CRACKIN'
HOW LONG, HOW LONG

Southern Man

Words and Music by Neil Young

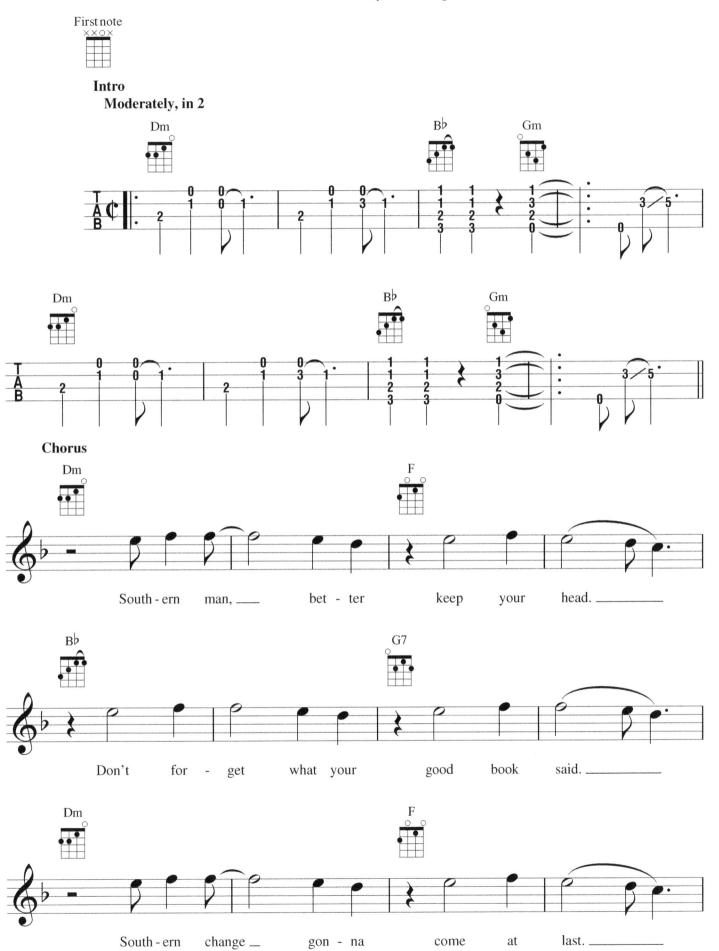

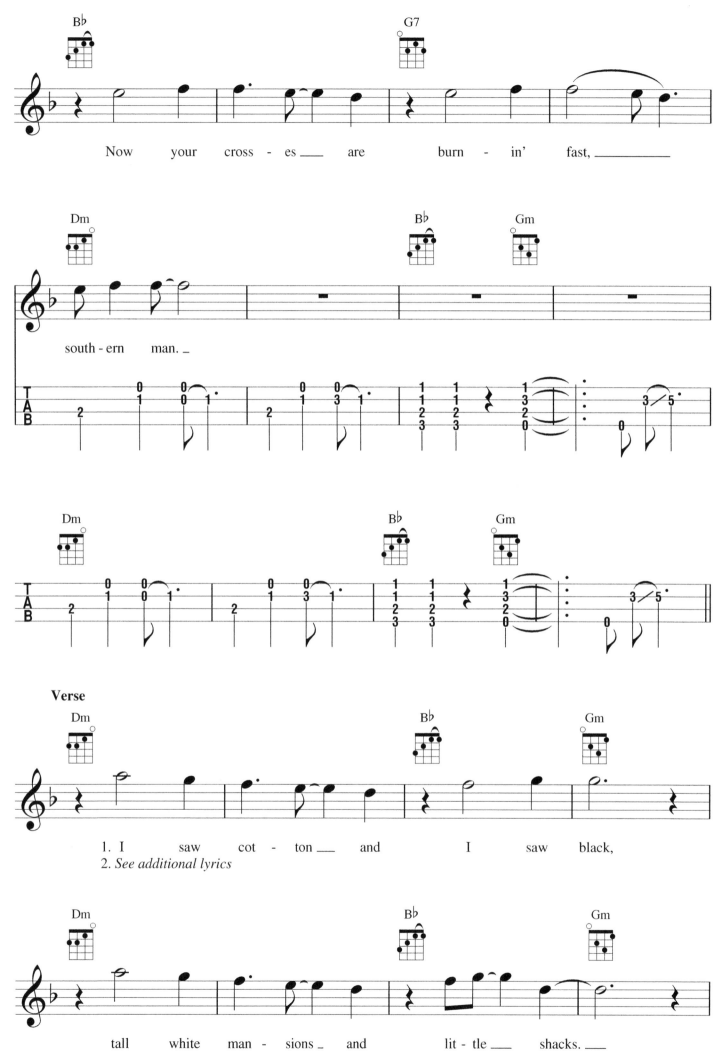

Now your cross - es ___ are burn - in' fast, _____

south - ern man. _

1. I saw cot - ton ___ and I saw black,

2. *See additional lyrics*

tall white man - sions _ and lit - tle ___ shacks. ___

South - ern man, ___ when will you pay them back?

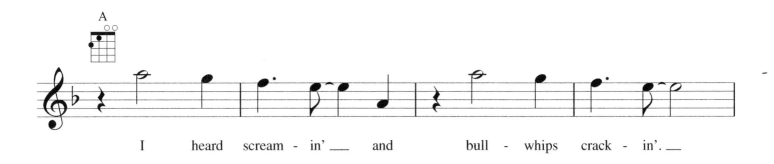

I heard scream - in' ___ and bull - whips crack - in'. ___

How long, how long? ___ Ah. _____

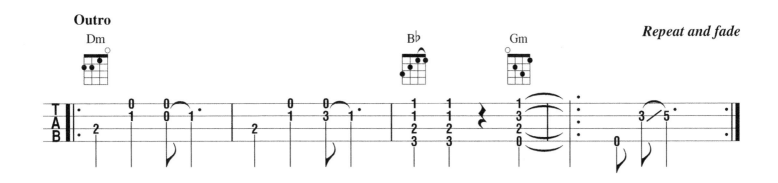

Outro

Repeat and fade

Additional Lyrics

2. Lily Belle, your hair is golden brown,
I've seen your black man comin' 'round.
Swear by God, I'm gonna cut him down!
I heard screamin' and bullwhips crackin'.
How long, how long? Ah.

CROSBY, STILLS, NASH & YOUNG
Ohio

Tin Soldiers and Nixon Coming
We're Finally On Our Own
This Summer I Hear the Drumming
Four Dead in Ohio
Gotta Get Down To It
Soldiers Are Cutting Us Down
Should Have Been Done Long Ago
What if You Knew Her and Found Her Dead
   on the Ground
How Can You Run When You Know?

Find the
Cost of Freedom

Find the Cost of Freedom
Buried in the Ground
Mother Earth Will Swallow You
Lay Your Body Down

BILL OF RIGHTS

ARTICLE I.

SEE PROTECTION OF CITI

OHIO

TIN SOLDIERS AND NIXON'S COMIN'
WE'RE FINALLY ON OUR OWN
THIS SUMMER I HEAR THE DRUMMIN'
FOUR DEAD IN OHIO

GOTTA GET DOWN TO IT
SOLDIERS ARE CUTTING US DOWN
SHOULD HAVE BEEN DONE LONG AGO
WHAT IF YOU KNEW HER AND FOUND HER DEAD ON THE GROUND
HOW CAN YOU RUN WHEN YOU KNOW

Ohio

Words and Music by Neil Young

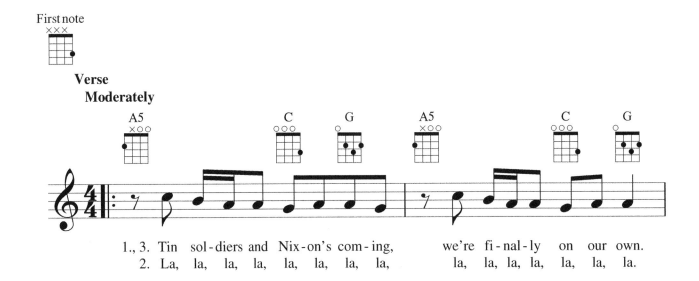

1., 3. Tin sol-diers and Nix-on's com-ing, we're fi-nal-ly on our own.
2. La, la, la, la, la, la, la, la, la, la, la, la, la, la, la.

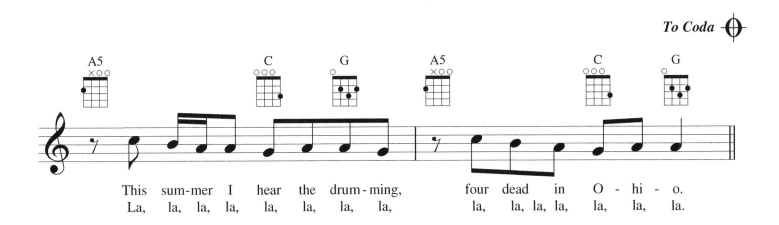

To Coda ⊕

This sum-mer I hear the drum-ming, four dead in O-hi-o.
La, la, la, la, la, la, la, la, la, la, la, la, la, la.

Chorus

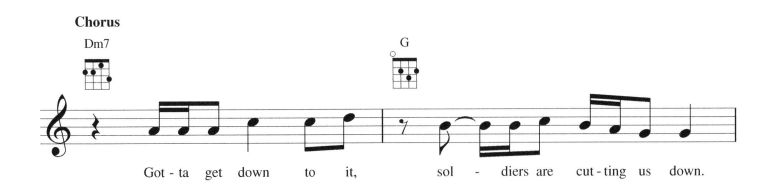

Got-ta get down to it, sol-diers are cut-ting us down.

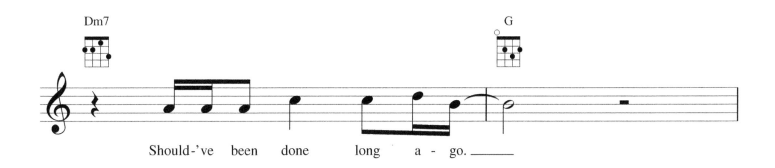

Should-'ve been done long a - go. ____

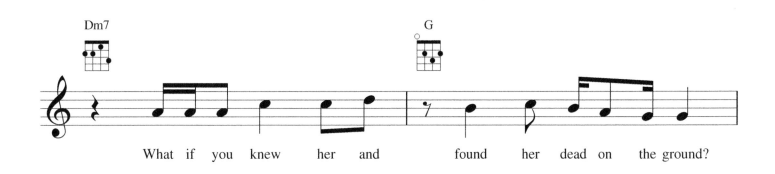

What if you knew her and found her dead on the ground?

2nd time, D.C. al Coda

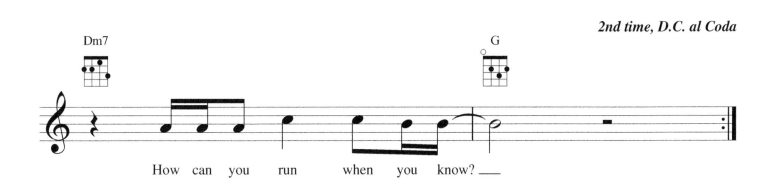

How can you run when you know? ___

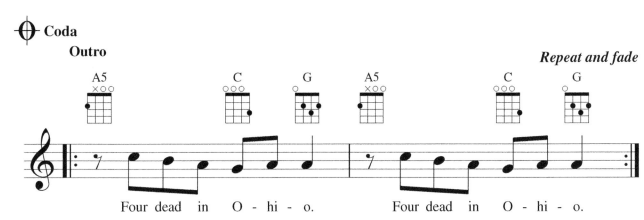

Four dead in O - hi - o. Four dead in O - hi - o.

THE NEEDLE & THE DAMAGE DONE

I CAUGHT YOU KNOCKING AT MY CELLAR DOOR
I LOVE YOU BABY CAN I HAVE SOME MORE
OOH, THE DAMAGE DONE
I HIT THE CITY AND I LOST MY BAND
I WATCHED THE NEEDLE TAKE ANOTHER MAN
GONE, GONE, THE DAMAGE DONE

I SING THE SONG BECAUSE I LOVE THE MAN
I KNOW THAT SOME OF YOU DON'T UNDERSTAND
MILK BLOOD TO KEEP FROM RUNNING OUT
I'VE SEEN THE NEEDLE AND THE DAMAGE DONE
A LITTLE PART OF IT IN EVERY ONE
BUT EVERY JUNKIE'S LIKE A SETTING SUN

The Needle and the Damage Done

Words and Music by Neil Young

1. I caught you knock - ing at my cel - lar door. __
3. *See additional lyrics*

I love you, ba - by, can I have some more? __ Ooh, _____

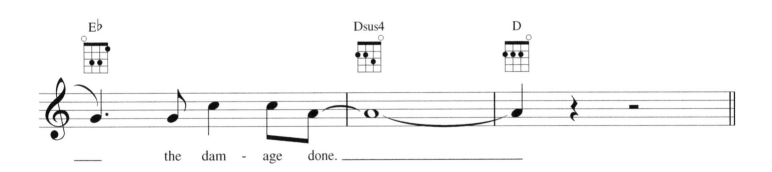

___ the dam - age done. _____

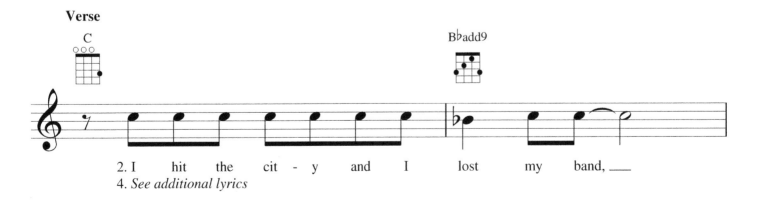

2. I hit the cit - y and I lost my band, __
4. *See additional lyrics*

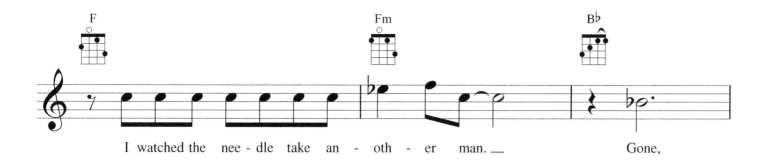

I watched the nee - dle take an - oth - er man. __ Gone,

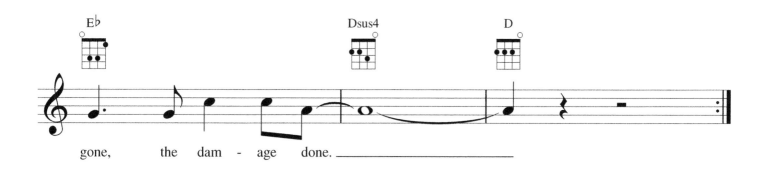

gone, the dam - age done. _____

Outro

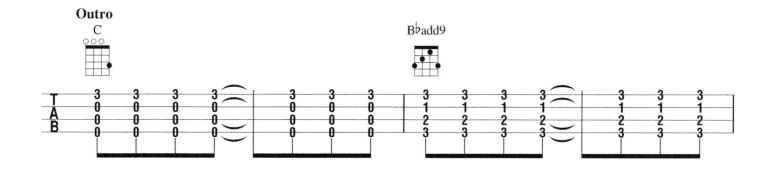

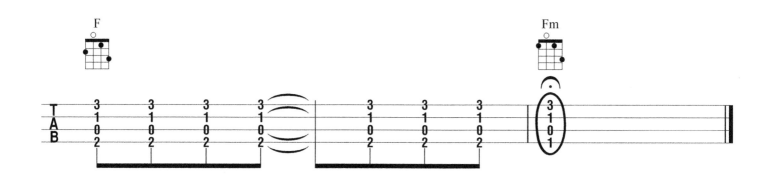

Additional Lyrics

3. I sing the song because I love the man,
   I know that some of you don't understand.
   Milk blood to keep from running out.

4. I've seen the needle and the damage done,
   A little part of it in everyone,
   But every junkie's like a setting sun.

Old Man

Old man look at my life, I'm a lot like you were
Old man look at my life, twenty four and there's so much more
Live alone in a paradise that makes me think of two.
Love lost, such a cost, give me things that don't get lost
Like a coin that won't get tossed
Rolling home to you.

Old man take a look at my life
I'm a lot like you.
I need someone to love me the whole day through
Ah, one look in my eyes and you can tell that's true.

Lullabys, look in your eyes, run around the same old town
Doesn't mean that much to me to mean that much to you
I've been first and last look at how the time goes past
But I'm all alone at last
Rolling home to you.

There's a World

How a world you're living in
Remember how you past
All got a children in the wind
Takes it in and blow it hard

OLD MAN

OLD MAN, LOOK AT MY LIFE
I'M A LOT LIKE YOU WERE
OLD MAN, LOOK AT MY LIFE
I'M A LOT LIKE YOU WERE

OLD MAN, LOOK AT MY LIFE
TWENTY FOUR AND THERE'S SO MUCH MORE
LIVE ALONE IN A PARADISE
THAT MAKES ME THINK OF TWO
LOVE LOST, SUCH A COST
GIVES ME THINGS THAT DON'T GET LOST
LIKE A COIN THAT WON'T GET TOSSED
ROLLING HOME TO YOU

OLD MAN, TAKE A LOOK AT MY LIFE, I'M A LOT LIKE YOU
I NEED SOMEONE TO LOVE ME THE WHOLE DAY THROUGH
OH, ONE LOOK IN MY EYES AND YOU CAN TELL THAT'S TRUE

LULLABIES, LOOK IN YOUR EYES
RUN AROUND THE SAME OLD TOWN
DOESN'T MEAN THAT MUCH TO ME
TO MEAN THAT MUCH TO YOU
I'VE BEEN FIRST AND LAST
LOOK AT HOW THE TIME GOES PAST
BUT I'M ALL ALONE AT LAST
ROLLING HOME TO YOU

OLD MAN, TAKE A LOOK AT MY LIFE, I'M A LOT LIKE YOU
I NEED SOMEONE TO LOVE ME THE WHOLE DAY THROUGH
OH, ONE LOOK IN MY EYES AND YOU CAN TELL THAT'S TRUE

OLD MAN, LOOK AT MY LIFE
I'M A LOT LIKE YOU WERE
OLD MAN, LOOK AT MY LIFE
I'M A LOT LIKE YOU WERE

Old Man

Words and Music by Neil Young

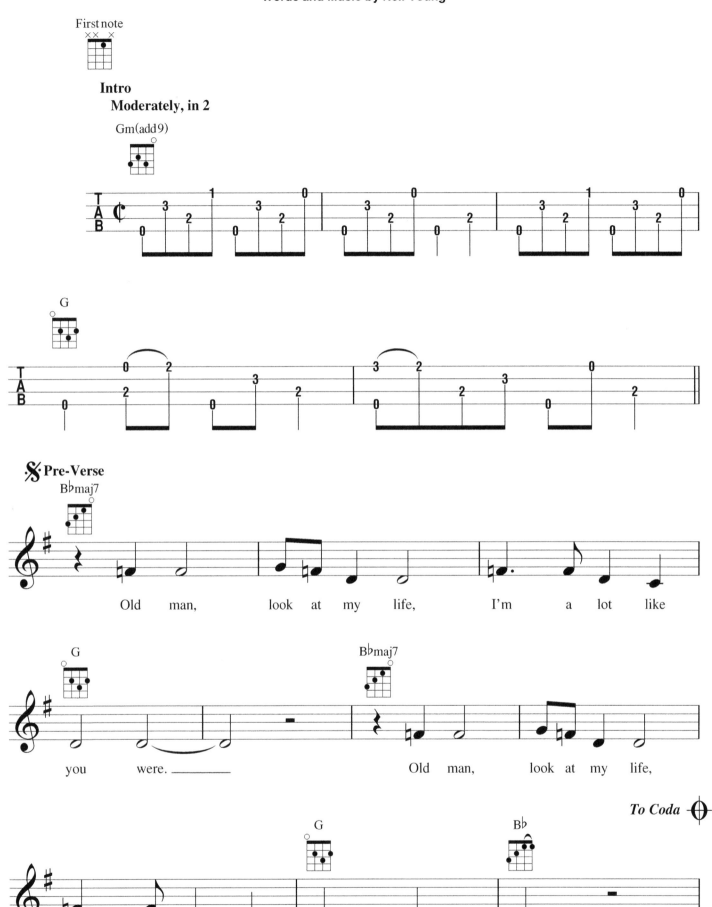

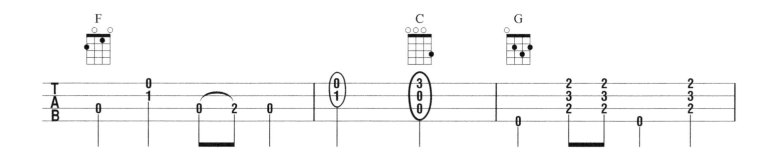

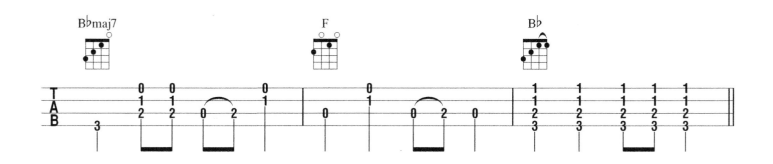

Verse

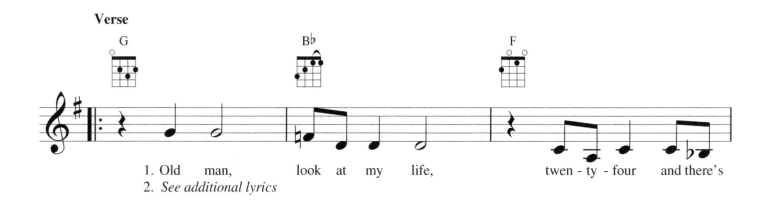

1. Old man, look at my life, twen - ty - four and there's
2. *See additional lyrics*

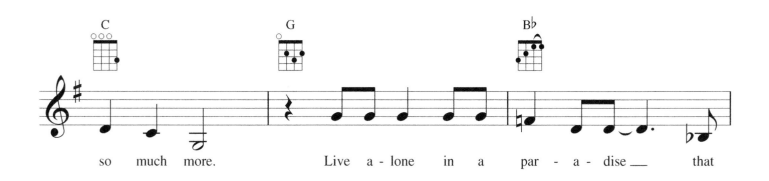

so much more. Live a - lone in a par - a - dise ___ that

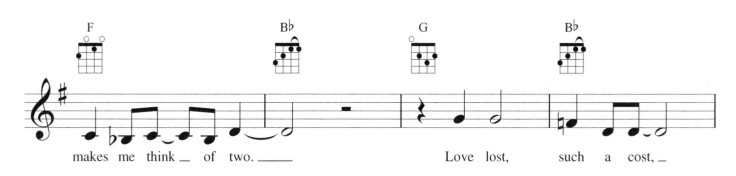

makes me think ___ of two. ___ Love lost, such a cost, ___

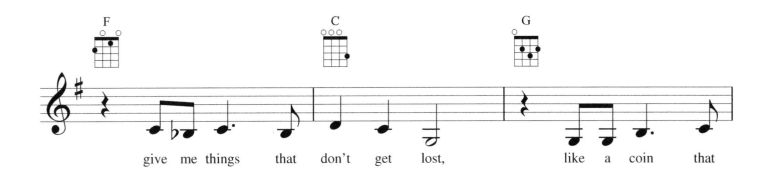

give me things that don't get lost, like a coin that

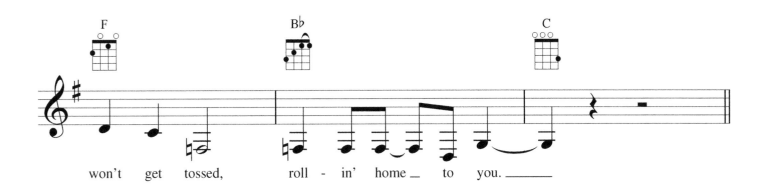

won't get tossed, roll - in' home __ to you. _____

Chorus

Old man, take a look at my life, __ I'm a lot _____ like __ you. __

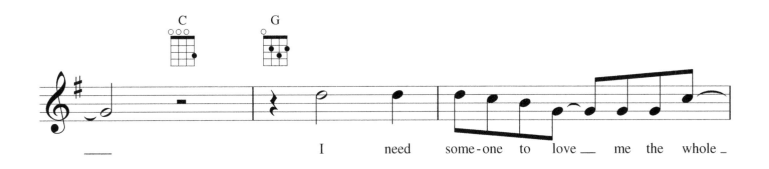

____ I need some-one to love __ me the whole __

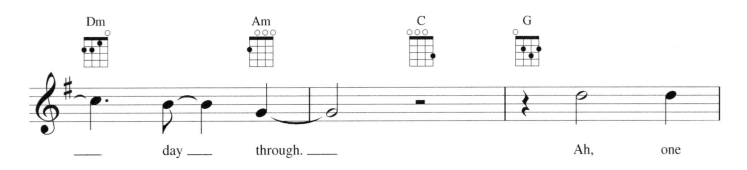

____ day ___ through. ____ Ah, one

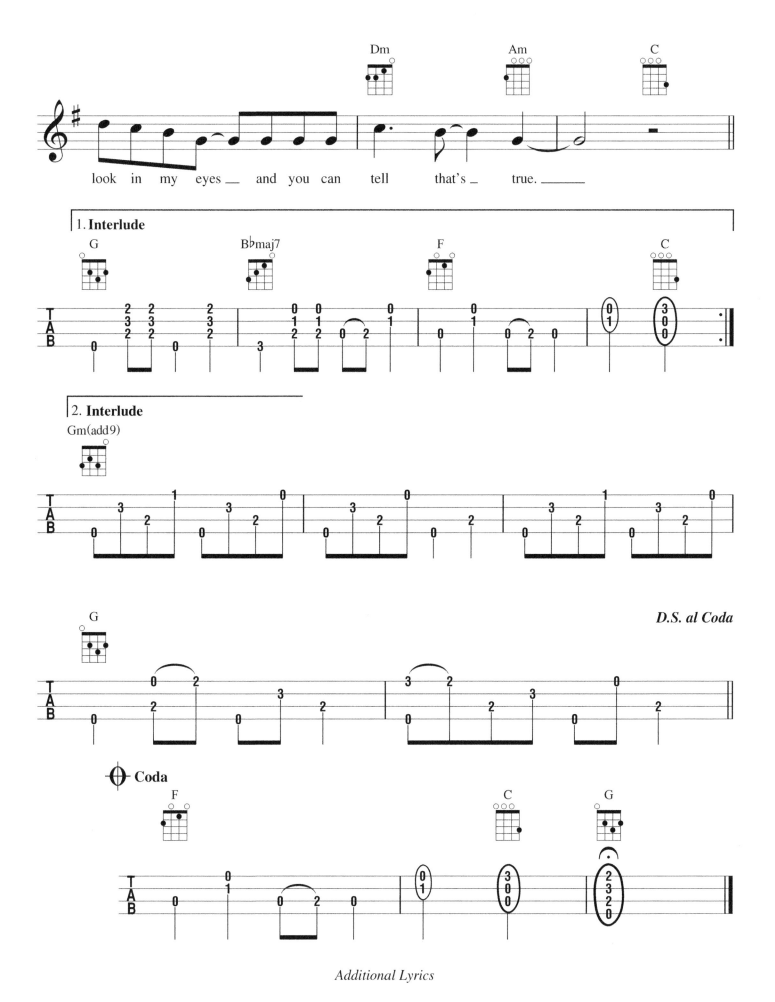

look   in   my   eyes ___   and   you   can   tell   that's ___   true. _____

1. Interlude

2. Interlude

D.S. al Coda

Coda

Additional Lyrics

2. Lullabies, look in your eyes, run around the same old town,
   Doesn't mean that much to me to mean that much to you.
   I've been first and last, look at how the time goes past,
   But I'm all alone at last, rollin' home to you.

HEART OF GOLD

I WANT TO LIVE
I WANT TO GIVE
I'VE BEEN A MINER FOR A HEART OF GOLD
IT'S THESE EXPRESSIONS
I NEVER GIVE
THAT KEEP ME SEARCHING FOR A HEART OF GOLD
AND I'M GETTING OLD
KEEP ME SEARCHING FOR A HEART OF GOLD
AND I'M GETTING OLD

I'VE BEEN TO HOLLYWOOD
I'VE BEEN TO REDWOOD
I CROSSED THE OCEAN FOR A HEART OF GOLD
I'VE BEEN IN MY MIND
IT'S SUCH A FINE LINE
THAT KEEPS ME SEARCHING FOR A HEART OF GOLD
AND I'M GETTING OLD
KEEPS ME SEARCHING FOR A HEART OF GOLD
AND I'M GETTING OLD

KEEP ME SEARCHING FOR A HEART OF GOLD
YOU KEEP ME SEARCHING
AND I'M GROWING OLD
KEEP ME SEARCHING FOR A HEART OF GOLD
I'VE BEEN A MINER FOR A HEART OF GOLD

Heart of Gold

Words and Music by Neil Young

First note

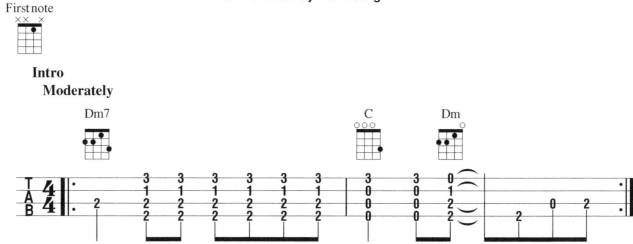

Intro
Moderately

Verse

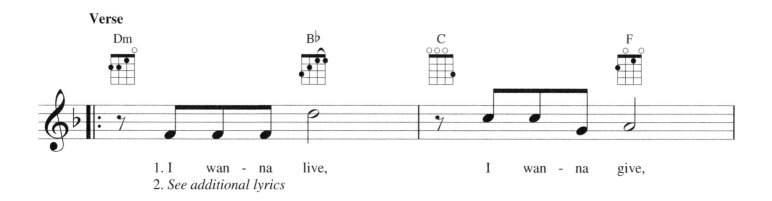

1. I wan - na live,   I wan - na give,
2. *See additional lyrics*

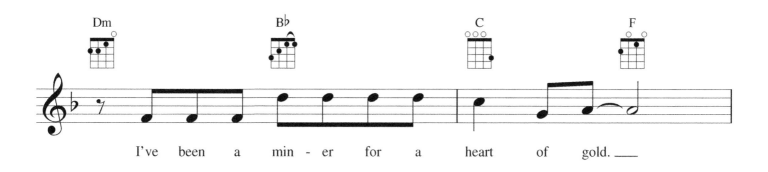

I've been a min - er for a heart of gold. ___

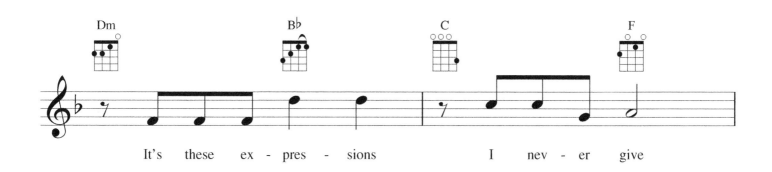

It's these ex - pres - sions I nev - er give

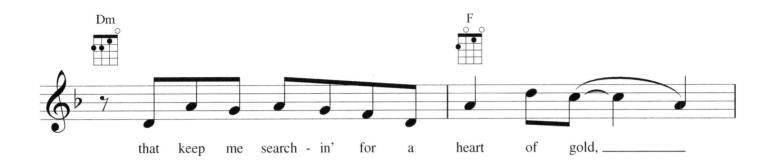

that keep me search - in' for a heart of gold, _____

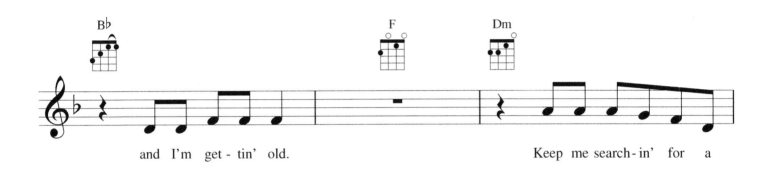

and I'm get - tin' old.   Keep me search - in' for a

heart of gold, _____   and I'm get - tin' old.

1. **Interlude**

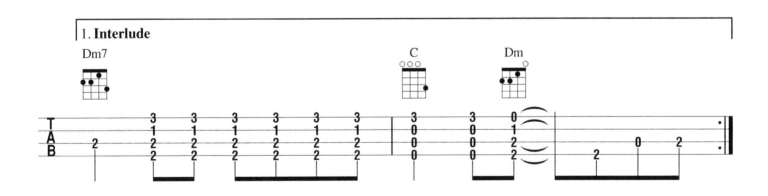

2.

Outro

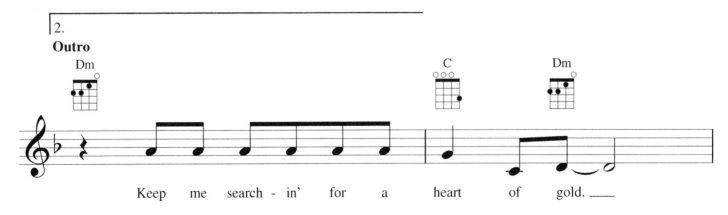

Keep me search - in' for a heart of gold. ____

You keep me search - in' and I'm grow - in' old. ____

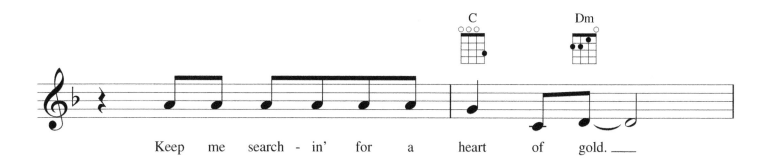

Keep me search - in' for a heart of gold. ____

I've been a min - er for a heart of gold. _____

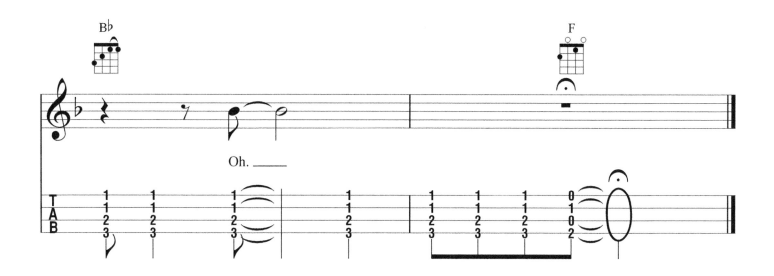

Oh. ____

Additional Lyrics

2. I've been to Hollywood, I've been to Redwood.
I crossed the ocean for a heart of gold.
I've been in my mind, it's such a fine line
That keeps me searchin' for a heart of gold,
And I'm gettin' old.
Keeps me searchin' for a heart of gold,
And I'm gettin' old.

LIKE A HURRICANE

ONCE I THOUGHT I SAW YOU IN A CROWDED HAZY BAR
DANCING ON THE LIGHT FROM STAR TO STAR
FAR ACROSS THE MOONBEAMS, I KNOW THAT'S WHO YOU ARE
I SAW YOUR BROWN EYES TURNING ONCE TO FIRE

YOU ARE LIKE A HURRICANE
THERE'S CALM IN YOUR EYE
AND I'M GETTING BLOWN AWAY
TO SOMEWHERE SAFER WHERE THE FEELINGS STAY
I WANT TO LOVE YOU BUT I'M GETTING BLOWN AWAY

I AM JUST A DREAMER, BUT YOU ARE JUST A DREAM
YOU COULD HAVE BEEN ANYONE TO ME
BEFORE THAT MOMENT YOU TOUCHED MY LIPS
THAT PERFECT FEELING WHEN TIME JUST SLIPS
AWAY BETWEEN US AND OUR FOGGY TRIPS

YOU ARE LIKE A HURRICANE
THERE'S CALM IN YOUR EYE
AND I'M GETTING BLOWN AWAY
TO SOMEWHERE SAFER WHERE THE FEELINGS STAY
I WANT TO LOVE YOU BUT I'M GETTING BLOWN AWAY

YOU ARE JUST A DREAMER, AND I AM JUST A DREAM
YOU COULD HAVE BEEN ANYONE TO ME
BEFORE THAT MOMENT YOU TOUCHED MY LIPS
THAT PERFECT FEELING WHEN TIME JUST SLIPS
AWAY BETWEEN US ON OUR FOGGY TRIP

YOU ARE LIKE A HURRICANE
THERE'S CALM IN YOUR EYE
AND I'M GETTING BLOWN AWAY
TO SOMEWHERE SAFER WHERE THE FEELINGS STAY
I WANT TO LOVE YOU BUT I'M GETTING BLOWN AWAY

Like a Hurricane

Words and Music by Neil Young

COMES A TIME

COMES A TIME WHEN YOU'RE DRIFTIN'
COMES A TIME WHEN YOU SETTLE DOWN
COMES A LIGHT, FEELIN'S LIFTIN'
LIFT THAT BABY RIGHT UP OFF THE GROUND

OH, THIS OLD WORLD KEEPS SPINNIN' ROUND
IT'S A WONDER TALL TREES AIN'T LAYIN' DOWN
THERE COMES A TIME

YOU AND I, WE WERE CAPTURED
WE TOOK OUR SOULS AND WE FLEW AWAY
WE WERE RIGHT, WE WERE GIVING
THAT'S HOW WE KEPT WHAT WE GAVE AWAY

OH, THIS OLD WORLD KEEPS SPINNIN' ROUND
IT'S A WONDER TALL TREES AIN'T LAYIN' DOWN
THERE COMES A TIME

THERE COMES A TIME
THERE COMES A TIME

(REPEAT)

Comes a Time

Words and Music by Neil Young

HEY HEY MY MY (INTO THE BLACK)

HEY HEY, MY MY
ROCK AND ROLL CAN NEVER DIE
THERE'S MORE TO THE PICTURE
THAN MEETS THE EYE
HEY HEY, MY MY

OUT OF THE BLUE AND INTO THE BLACK
YOU PAY FOR THIS, BUT THEY GIVE YOU THAT
AND ONCE YOU'RE GONE, YOU CAN'T COME BACK
WHEN YOU'RE OUT OF THE BLUE AND INTO THE BLACK

THE KING IS GONE BUT HE'S NOT FORGOTTEN
IS THIS THE STORY OF JOHNNY ROTTEN?
IT'S BETTER TO BURN OUT 'CAUSE RUST NEVER SLEEPS
THE KING IS GONE BUT HE'S NOT FORGOTTEN

HEY HEY, MY MY
ROCK AND ROLL CAN NEVER DIE
THERE'S MORE TO THE PICTURE
THAN MEETS THE EYE

Hey Hey, My My
(Into the Black)
Words and Music by Neil Young

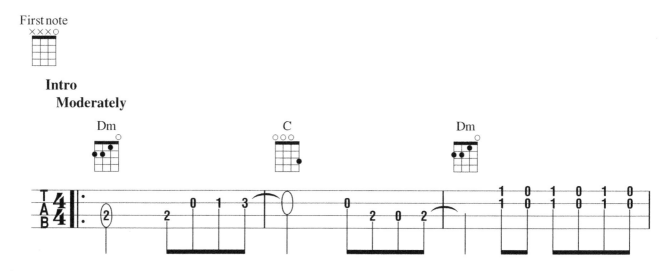

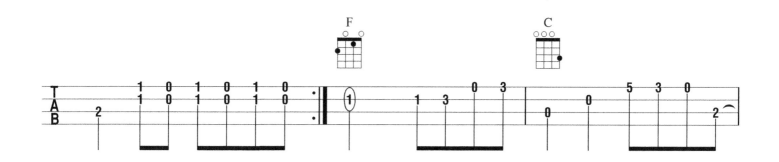

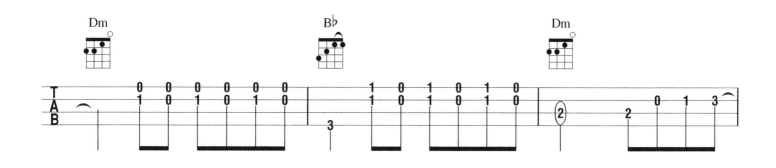

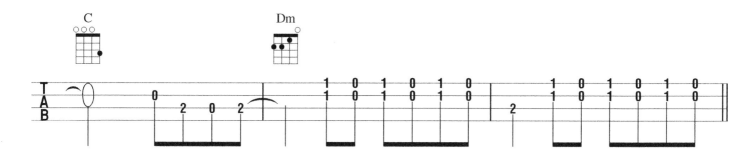

§ **Verse**

1., 4. Hey hey, _____ my my. _____
2., 3. *See additional lyrics*

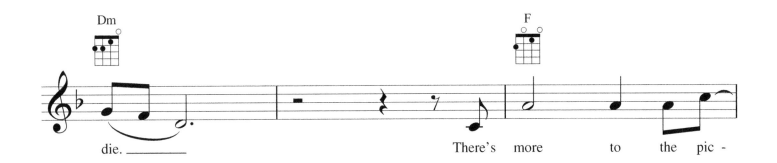

Rock and roll can nev - er

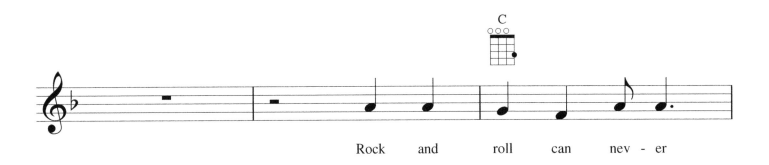

die. _____ There's more to the pic -

To Coda ⊕

- ture than meets the eye. _____

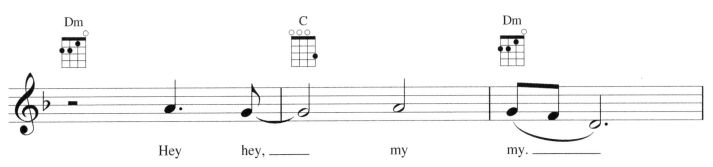

Hey hey, _____ my my. _____

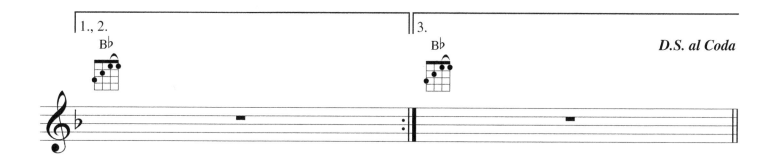

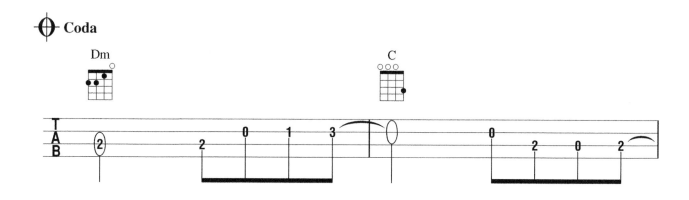

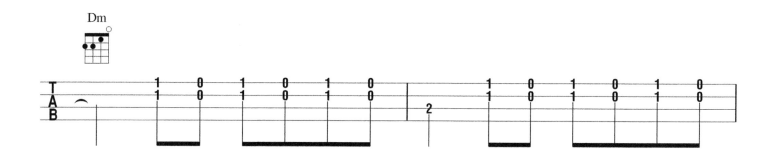

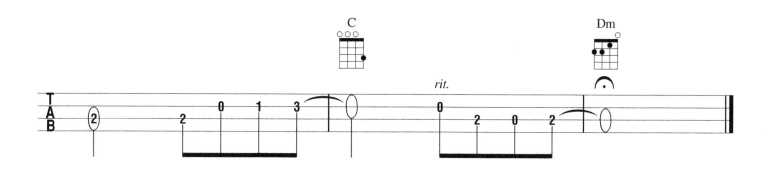

Additional Lyrics

2. Out of the blue and into the black,
   You pay for this, but they give you that.
   And once you're gone, you can't come back,
   When you're out of the blue and into the black.

3. The king is gone, but he's not forgotten.
   Is this the story of Johnny Rotten?
   It's better to burn out, 'cause rust never sleeps.
   The king is gone, but he's not forgotten.

61

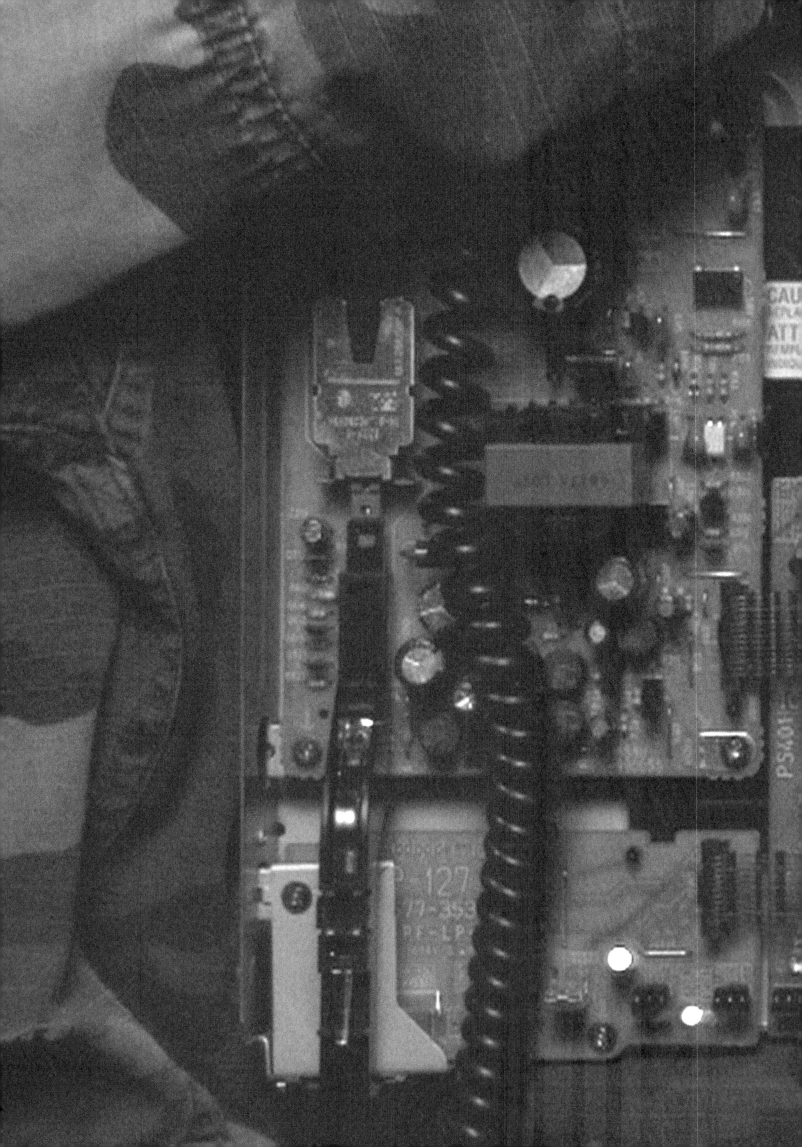

ROCKIN' IN THE FREE WORLD

THERE'S COLORS ON THE STREET
RED, WHITE AND BLUE
PEOPLE SHUFFLIN' THEIR FEET
PEOPLE SLEEPIN' IN THEIR SHOES
BUT THERE'S A WARNIN' SIGN
ON THE ROAD AHEAD
THERE'S A LOT OF PEOPLE SAYIN'
WE'D BE BETTER OFF DEAD
DON'T FEEL LIKE SATAN
BUT I AM TO THEM
SO I TRY TO FORGET IT
ANY WAY I CAN

KEEP ON ROCKIN' IN THE FREE WORLD (4X)

I SEE A WOMAN IN THE NIGHT
WITH A BABY IN HER HAND
NEAR AN OLD STREET LIGHT
NEAR A GARBAGE CAN
NOW SHE'S PUT THE KID AWAY
AND SHE'S GONE TO GET A HIT
SHE HATES HER LIFE
AND WHAT SHE'S DONE TO IT
THAT'S ONE MORE KID
THAT'LL NEVER GO TO SCHOOL
NEVER GET TO FALL IN LOVE
NEVER GET TO BE COOL

KEEP ON ROCKIN' IN THE FREE WORLD (4X)

WE GOT A THOUSAND POINTS OF LIGHT
FOR THE HOMELESS MAN
WE GOT A KINDER, GENTLER
MACHINE-GUN HAND
WE GOT DEPARTMENT STORES
AND TOILET PAPER
GOT STYROFOAM BOXES
FOR THE OZONE LAYER
GOT A MAN OF THE PEOPLE
SAYS KEEP HOPE ALIVE
GOT FUEL TO BURN
GOT ROADS TO DRIVE

KEEP ON ROCKIN' IN THE FREE WORLD (4X)

Rockin' in the Free World

Words and Music by Neil Young

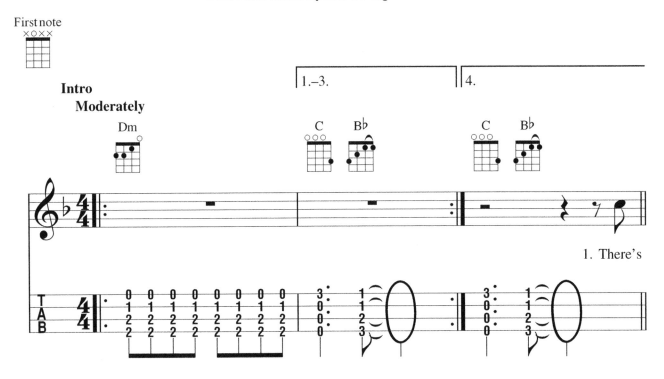

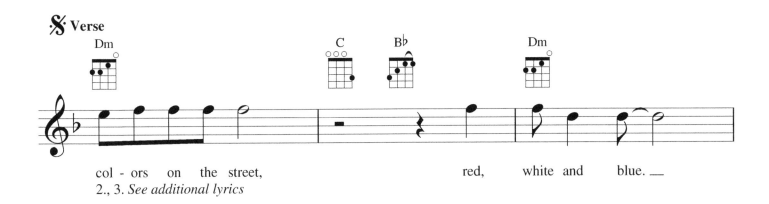

col - ors on the street,
2., 3. *See additional lyrics*

red, white and blue. ___

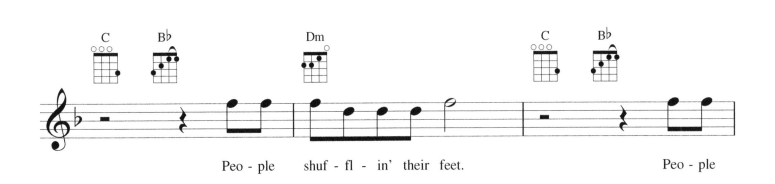

Peo - ple shuf - fl - in' their feet.

Peo - ple

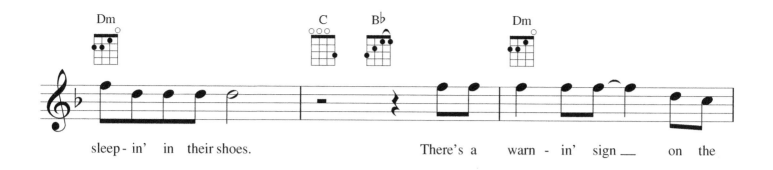

sleep - in' in their shoes.   There's a   warn - in' sign ___ on the

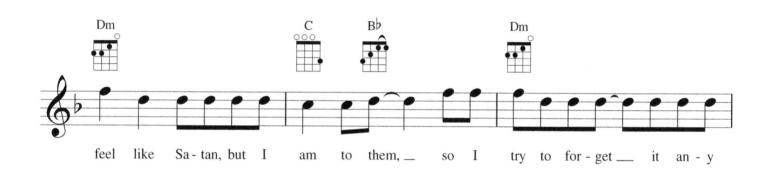

road   a - head. ___ There's a   lot of peo - ple say - in' we'd be   bet - ter off   dead. Don't

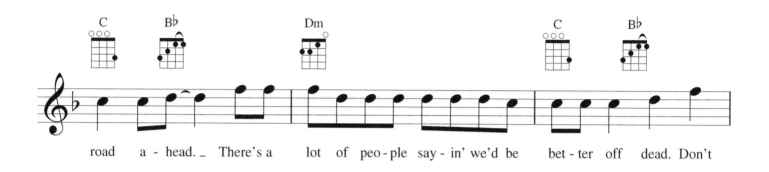

feel like Sa - tan, but I   am   to them, ___   so I   try to for - get ___ it an - y

Chorus

way   I   can. ___   Keep on rock - in' in   the   free   world.

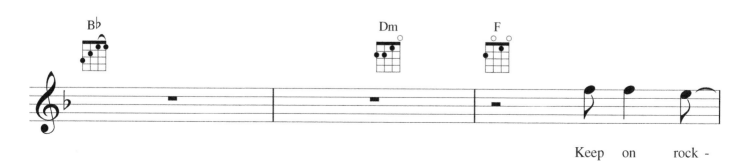

Keep   on   rock -

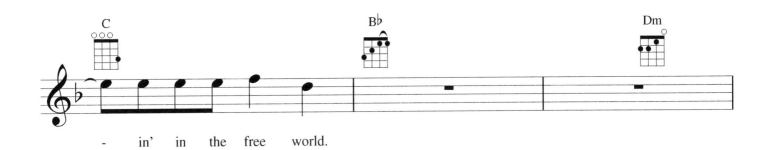

- in' in the free world.

Keep on rock - in' in the free world.

Keep on rock - in' in the free world.

Interlude

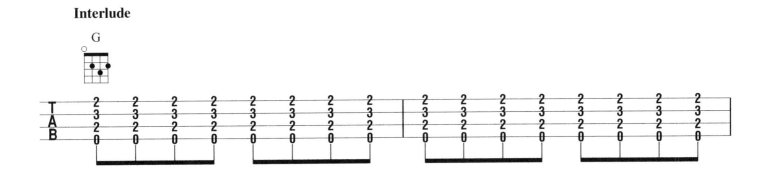

To Coda 1

To Coda 2

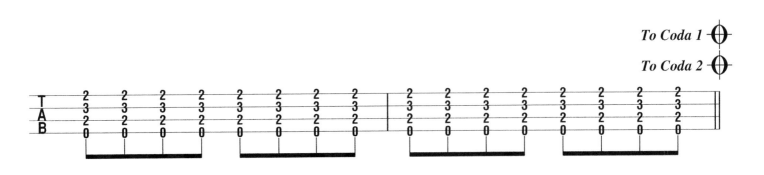

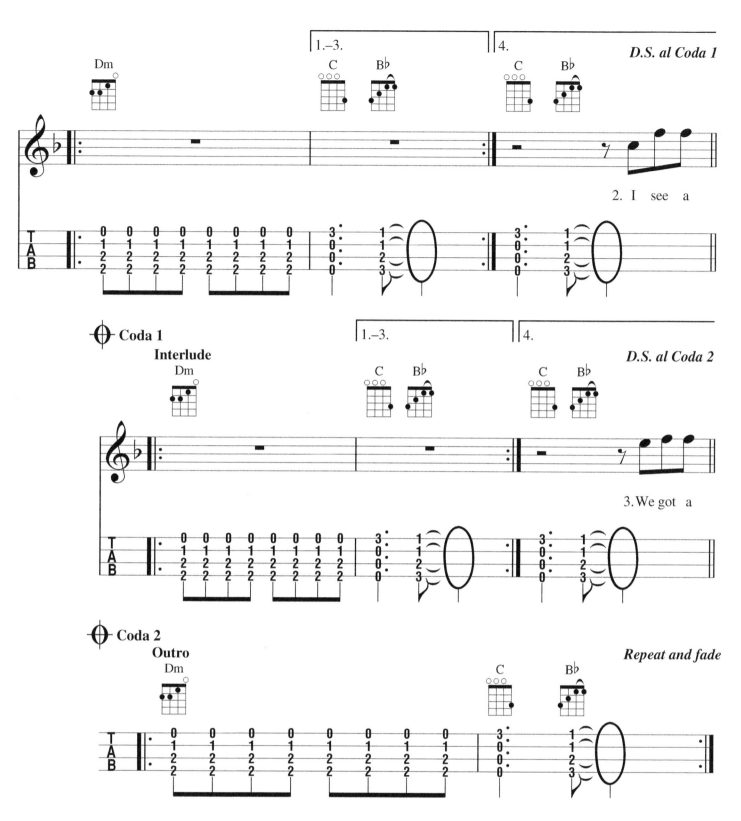

Additional Lyrics

2. I see a woman in the night with a baby in her hand.
   There's an old street light near a garbage can.
   Now she puts the kid away and she's gone to get a hit.
   She hates her life and what she's done to it.
   There's one more kid that'll never go to school,
   Never get to fall in love, never get to be cool.

3. We got a thousand points of light for the homeless man.
   We got a kinder, gentler machine gun hand.
   We got department stores and toilet paper.
   Got styrofoam boxes for the ozone layer.
   Got a man of the people, says keep hope alive.
   Got fuel to burn, got roads to drive.

HARVEST MOON

COME A LITTLE BIT CLOSER
HEAR WHAT I HAVE TO SAY
JUST LIKE CHILDREN SLEEPING
WE COULD DREAM THIS NIGHT AWAY

BUT THERE'S A FULL MOON RISING
LET'S GO DANCING IN THE LIGHT
WE KNOW WHERE THE MUSIC'S PLAYING
LET'S GO OUT AND FEEL THE NIGHT

BECAUSE I'M STILL IN LOVE WITH YOU
I WANT TO SEE YOU DANCE AGAIN
BECAUSE I'M STILL IN LOVE WITH YOU
ON THIS HARVEST MOON

WHEN WE WERE STRANGERS
I WATCHED YOU FROM AFAR
WHEN WE WERE LOVERS
I LOVED YOU WITH ALL MY HEART

BUT NOW IT'S GETTING LATE
AND THE MOON IS CLIMBING HIGH
I WANT TO CELEBRATE
SEE IT SHINING IN YOUR EYE

BECAUSE I'M STILL IN LOVE WITH YOU
I WANT TO SEE YOU DANCE AGAIN
BECAUSE I'M STILL IN LOVE WITH YOU
ON THIS HARVEST MOON

Harvest Moon

Words and Music by Neil Young

Pre-Chorus

But there's a full moon ris - in'; let's go danc -
But now it's get - tin' late ___ and the moon ___

- in' in ___ the light. ___
___ is climb - in' high. ___

We know where the
I want to

mu - sic's play - in'; let's go out ___ and feel the night. _
cel - e - brate, _ see the shin - in' in your eyes. _

Chorus

Be - cause I'm still in love ___ with

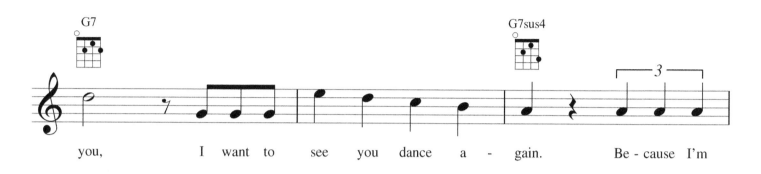

you, I want to see you dance a - gain. Be - cause I'm

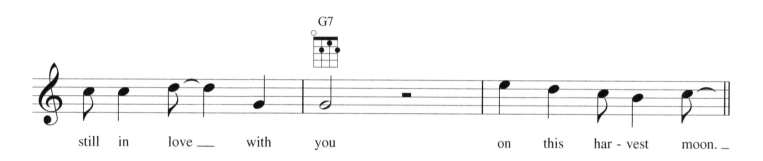

still in love ___ with you on this har - vest moon. ___

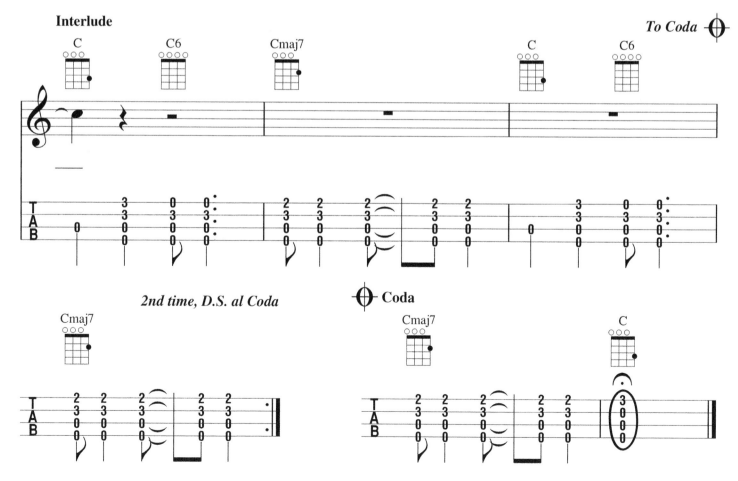

Interlude

To Coda

2nd time, D.S. al Coda

Coda

ORIGINAL MASTER TAPES TRANSFERRED BY JOHN NOWLAND AT REDWOOD DIGITAL, WOODSIDE, CA
DIGITALLY MASTERED BY TIM MULLIGAN AT REDWOOD DIGITAL
ASSISTING ENGINEER AT REDWOOD DIGITAL: JOHN HAUSMANN
SENIOR TECHNICAL ENGINEER AT REDWOOD DIGITAL: HARRY SITAM
FOR RECORDING TECHNICAL NOTES AND ADDITIONAL INFORMATION GO TO
WWW.NEILYOUNG.COM/ARCHIVES

DIRECTION: ELLIOT ROBERTS, LOOKOUT MANAGEMENT
COVER PHOTO: JOEL BERNSTEIN
ART DIRECTION & DESIGN: GARY BURDEN & JENICE HEO FOR R. TWERK & CO.,
TOSHI ONUKI, L.A. JOHNSON & NEIL YOUNG FOR SHAKEY PICTURES.
CAMERA: JARID JOHNSON. GRIP: WILL MITCHELL.

THANKS TO PEGI.

SONGBOOK ART DIRECTION AND DESIGN: GARY BURDEN AND JENICE HEO FOR R TWERK & CO
SONGBOOK PRODUCTION DESIGN: JESSE BURDEN

®©2004 REPRISE RECORDS. MADE IN U.S.A. 48935-2